The Divine Romance - The Song of Jesus and His Bride

David River

Copyright © 2008 by David River

The Divine Romance - The Song of Jesus and His Bride
by David River

Printed in the United States of America

ISBN 978-1-60647-116-6

All rights reserved solely by the author. The author guarantees all contents are original and do not infringe upon the legal rights of any other person or work. No part of this book may be reproduced in any form without the permission of the author. The views expressed in this book are not necessarily those of the publisher.

Unless otherwise indicated, Bible quotations are taken from The Message version of the Bible. Copyright © 2005 by NavPress.

www.xulonpress.com

ಬಿ *Contents* ಅ

Dedication		vii
Theme		Zephaniah 3:17 viii
Introduction		A Love Story ix
Song 1	The Groom	The Battle for My Bride.............................17
Song 2	The Bride	Made to Love You..........21
Song 3	The Groom	Come Closer..................25
Song 4	The Bride	Open My Eyes 29
Song 5	The Groom	Love Endures Forever..33
Song 6	The Bride	Dream Maker 35
Song 7	The Groom	Without You 39
Song 8	The Bride	The Only Living God....43
Song 9	The Groom	Out of My Mind............47
Song 10	The Bride	God's Voice....................51
Song 11	The Groom	A Lifetime of Love 55
Song 12	The Bride	Amazing Love...............59
Song 13	The Groom	Safe................................63
Song 14	The Bride	The Heart of a Lion......67
Song 15	The Groom	If You Would Give Me This Dance 71
Song 16	The Bride	Lost in You....................75
Song 17	The Groom	Heaven on Earth 77
Song 18	The Bride	Savior 81

Song 19	*The Groom*	*Eternity..........................85*
Song 20	*The Bride*	*You are Love.................87*
Song 21	*The Groom*	*Heaven in Your Eyes....91*
Song 22	*The Bride*	*My Heart Let Me Find You........................95*
Song 23	*The Groom*	*The Wedding Rehearsal: The Look Says It All.....99*
Song 24	*The Bride*	*The Vows: I Belong to You............103*
Song 25	*Both Singing*	*The Marriage: Intimacy.......................107*
A New Song		*Psalm 96:1-4...............111*

To Jesus Christ: The King of Lovers
Open Our Ears to Hear Your Song

To His Bride: The Church
May You Find the Love You're Longing for in Him

The Lord your God is with you,
He is mighty to save.
He will take great delight in you,
He will quiet you with His love,
He will rejoice over you with singing.

Zephaniah 3:17 (NIV)

Introduction
෨ *A Love Story* ෧

Since the dawn of creation, God has had a dream that has spanned millenniums, conquered countries, mended the broken and directed the course of history. It is a dream for which saints have searched, prophets have prayed and disciples have died. It is the dream above all other dreams, a vision yet unfulfilled.

What is this mysterious dream that countless people throughout history have sought? The answer is actually very simple. It is so easily understood that children grasp the concept. For remember, those who come to God must have the faith of a child. If you currently have a small child, all you have to do is look on their bookshelf to find the illusive answer to this puzzling question.

What is God's dream? God's dream is to orchestrate a divine romance between His Son Jesus and you as His bride. Much like a romantic fairytale, for centuries God has been writing and directing a grand saga about a knight, a dragon, and a maiden in distress. God dreams of love and romance the way knights used to dream of rescuing a princess. Am I stretching my imagination too much? Then ponder this for a moment.

As far back as Eden God has been writing an everlasting love story: from Adam and Eve, to Jacob and Rachel, to Solomon and his bride, all the way up to the return of Jesus to sweep away His own bride to the grand wedding celebration in heaven. And all throughout history God has hinted about this romance between Jesus and you as His bride, through the prophets and Biblical stories.

In Isaiah, God said, "As a bridegroom rejoices over his bride, so your God will rejoice over you" (Isaiah 62:5, NIV). Stop and think about that for a moment. Remember that Jacob and Rachel were chaste and had waited quite some time to be married. Jacob served years to make Rachel his wife. I imagine that their love was so deep and genuine that even storybooks could not depict its depth. How do you think Jacob must have felt on their wedding day after serving all this time for her? Overjoyed? Delirious? This is how God rejoices over you.

Hosea also illustrates the divine romance when he says that God will pursue and restore His people the way a bridegroom pursues a bride. "And now, here's what I am going to do: I'm going to start all over again. I'm taking her back out into the wilderness where we had our first date, and I'll court her. I'll give her bouquets of roses. I'll turn Heartbreak

Valley into Acres of Hope. She'll respond like she did as a young girl, those days when she was fresh out of Egypt. At that time" – this is God's message still – "you'll address me, 'Dear husband!' Never again will you address me, 'My slave-master!' And then I'll marry you for good – forever! I'll marry you true and proper, in love and tenderness. Yes, I'll marry you and neither leave you nor let you go. You'll come to know me, God, for who I really am" (Hosea 2:14-16, 19-20). Did you have any idea that God was so romantic?

John the Baptist also understood the romance between Jesus and His bride when in John 3:28-29 he said that he was baptizing the bride, that Jesus was the bridegroom, and that he himself was the friend of the bridegroom. John understood his role in God's grand scheme of things. He was the best man and he was preparing the bride for the arrival of the groom.

In Ephesians 5:31-32 Paul is speaking about the relationship between husbands and wives and he says this, "For this reason a man will leave his father and mother and be united with his wife, and the two will become one flesh. This is a profound mystery – but I am talking about Christ and the church." The relationship of husband and wife not only forms the foundation of our society going back to Adam and Eve, but according to Paul it also forms the foundation of the gospel. He makes it clear. Jesus is the husband. The church is His wife.

Finally in Revelation 19, John had a vision of the future and essentially what he saw was Jesus as a knight on a white horse with a sword returning to rescue His bride from a dragon. John foresaw the marriage of the lamb. Here's how he described it: "Then I heard what sounded like a great multitude, like the roar of rushing waters and like loud peals of thunder, shouting: 'Hallelujah! For our Lord God Almighty reigns. Let us rejoice and be glad and give Him glory! For the wedding of the Lamb has come, and His bride has made herself ready. Fine linen, bright and clean, was given her to wear.'" (Fine linen stands for the righteous acts of the saints.) "Then the angel said to me, 'Write: Blessed are those who are invited to the wedding supper of the Lamb'" (Revelation 19:6-9, NIV)!

So you see, God is the original romantic dreamer. The whole concept of a captive maiden who becomes a bride, a Knight who rescues her and becomes her Bridegroom, a dragon who is ultimately defeated, and a glorious wedding were all God's ideas from the beginning. Since the dawn of creation God has had this same dream and He wrote a love letter to help you discover it. And until you see the Bible and Christianity in this light, you will never fully comprehend them.

To prove how much God values love and romance, He included the Song of Solomon in the Bible. Solomon's song is also unquestionably the most romantic book in the entire Bible. And most agree that the love relationship that Solomon had with his bride is an allegory of Jesus and His bride. Since this is true, maybe we should search the Song of Solomon for some clues of how to love like Jesus.

Solomon opens his song by saying, "The Song – best of all songs – Solomon's song." He states this to tell us that what we are about to read was at one time actually a song. It's not just black letters on a white page. At one time his words had a beautiful melody that wooed the heart. Think of one of your favorite love songs that deeply stirs you. Solomon's song would have been equally if not more captivating.

As you continue reading the lyric, you might notice that it isn't just Solomon singing. Because of this his song might have been better titled, *The Song of Solomon and His Bride*, for both parties are actually singing. Another thing you may notice is a pattern that flows throughout the book: Solomon introduces the song, then his bride sings, then Solomon sings, then his bride sings again. This pattern is repeated throughout the entire song.

The Divine Romance was written with this inspiration in mind. You will discover that the first song in this book is Jesus singing over His bride (the church), while the second song is the church singing to Jesus. Like the Song of Solomon, the pattern is repeated until the culmination is reached by the marriage of the Lamb and His bride. Since this book is based upon the Song of Solomon, I have taken artistic liberties when referring to Jesus and the church in order to deliver romantic imagery. In other words, I have attributed humanlike emotions to Jesus as a groom and the church as a bride which one might not normally consider. I have taken these liberties to convey that Jesus is passionate about a bride, for He has anticipated their wedding for two thousand years. And in case you wonder, yes, I wrote all the songs from both perspectives: Jesus the Groom, and also His bride.

As you read this collection of love songs, I would encourage you to read them as a devotional - one song a day - as you allow Jesus' love to permeate your heart. Don't simply read it; meditate on it. Read each song two or three times as you picture Jesus singing over you. Sense His love drawing your heart into a deep intimacy with Him. When read in this fashion, you will discover anew the height, depth, length and breadth of His extravagant love for you. And in experiencing His love, you will be compelled to surrender your heart in complete abandonment to Him, for you are cherished like no other. You are the bride of Christ.

*Then I heard what sounded like a great multitude,
like the roar of rushing waters and like
loud peals of thunder, shouting:
"Hallelujah! For our Lord God Almighty reigns.
Let us rejoice and be glad and give Him glory!
For the wedding of the Lamb has come,
and His bride has made herself ready."*

Revelation 19:6-7 (NIV)

Song 1

ཎ *The Battle for My Bride* ༄
Jesus Singing over His Bride

I will search the mountains, the valleys,
the hills and the plains
For My bride is a beauty; with Me will she reign
I will look to the heavens, for there she was born
From My flesh she was taken, from Me she was torn
I have been through the wilderness,
but now I am free
O proud dragon it's useless fighting with Me
For I am a warrior and I trust in the great I AM
And you were defeated long before time began
Your foul breath, it no longer scares Me
Your threats are impotent;
you were overcome on the tree
I will slay you and I will surely cut you down
I will find her and place upon her head a crown
You cannot keep her hidden much longer
For my Father's power is mighty and much stronger
She is My princess and My queen to be
And I will marry her; just you wait and see
Once she was lost, but soon she will be found
For in your chains she is no longer bound
And when she is, the world will watch in wonder
Underneath the magnificent stars they will ponder
Then their eyes will be opened from all their pain
And from their hearts will fall all their chains
Dragon, you are defeated; your time's at an end

Soon you will be banished; to hell will I send
For this is your penalty and this is your prize
For your great deception and your great pride
And from there you will weep and gnash your teeth
As you see My beauty dancing with Me
For she is My angel and she is My bride
Forever she will be with Me, near Me, by My side
She is My beauty, and she is My queen
Together we will proclaim our love for Father
For He is supreme

*So I got up, went out and roved the city,
hunting through streets and down alleys.
I wanted my lover in the worst way.
I looked high and low, and didn't find him.*

Song of Solomon 3:2

Song 2

ஜ *Made to Love You* ௳
The Bride Singing to Jesus

I searched the world over
Craving, needing something more
Throwing off all constraints
My heart was trampled to the floor

Chasing after worldly dreams
Sure they would satisfy
I was left all alone
In the wilderness to cry

I searched mountains and valleys
And came to understand
Earthly dreams are vanity
A chasing after the wind

Dreams of fame and fortune
Of possessing material things
Could never truly compare
To the glory of knowing the King

For what do I have without You?
On earth what can satisfy
These longings in my soul
The yearnings of my heart's cry?

For Who do I have in heaven?
And where on earth can I turn?
All these dreams now surrendered
For You my heart eternally burns

I searched the world over
And now I finally see
My heart was made to love You
And Your love has set me free

Come with me from Lebanon, my bride.
Leave Lebanon behind, and come.

Song of Solomon 4:8

Song 3

ᛊ *Come Closer* ᛈ
Jesus Singing over His Bride

Come closer, come closer
Whisper your dreams in My ear
Don't run away and hide
Don't tremble in fear
I am just a King who loves you
Isn't this clear?

Come closer, come closer
Take Me by the hand
Together we will sing and
Dance throughout the land
While we dream of the wedding
So gloriously grand

Come closer, come closer
Why must you run and hide?
On the wings of angels
We will soar, we will glide
Surely you can see
I need you by my side

Surrender, surrender
I promise in all I do
To give you my Spirit
To make all your dreams come true
But first you must have the faith to believe
That I'll always love you

Restless in bed and sleepless through the night,
I longed for my lover.
I wanted him desperately,
His absence was painful.

Song of Solomon 3:1

Song 4

✧ *Open My Eyes* ✧
The Bride Singing to Jesus

Open my heart and lead me home
To these dreams of love
These dreams of love

Open my ears and let me hear
The beauty of Your voice
Your beautiful voice

Open my life and let me know
The mysteries of Your heart
Mysteries of Your heart

Open my soul and take all of me
I long to be Yours alone
To be Yours alone

Open my ears and let me hear You say
That I belong to You
I belong to You

Open my heart and lead me home
To feel Your warm embrace
Feel Your warm embrace

Open my life and take all of me
My heart is fully Yours
Heart is fully Yours

Open my eyes and lead me home
To Your kingdom come
Your kingdom come

Open my eyes and let me see
The perfection of Your face
Your perfect face

*Floodwaters can't drown love,
torrents of rain can't put it out.
Love can't be bought, love can't be sold.*

Song of Solomon 8:7

Song 5

❧ *Love Endures Forever* ❧
Jesus Singing over His Bride

You may lose your friends
You may lose your dreams
You may even lose your material things
Some may turn against you
but they can't take this one thing
The love of God will always remain
His love endures forever and it will never end

Your heart may break but He can make you sing
Even if you are standing alone in the pouring rain
Turn on the music and let go of your pain
His love flows to take away your stains
The love of God will always remain
His love endures forever and it will never end

God's love imitates a wedding ring
There is no beginning and there is no end
The circle continues though you stumble and sin
His love flows like a song you sing
The love of God will always remain
His love endures forever and it will never end

Look around you: Winter is over;
the winter rains are over, gone!
Spring flowers are in blossom all over.
The whole world's a choir - and singing!

Song of Solomon 2:11-12

Song 6

ᛒ *Dream Maker* ᛞ
The Bride Singing to Jesus

*In the depths of my cold winter
When the snow is falling down
When my dreams seem frozen
Like the snow upon the ground*

*I'll look to the heavens
And put my trust in You
Knowing that You have the power
To make my dreams come true*

*While I'm waiting for this winter
To melt the snow into spring
I'll stand in this valley
Raise my voice to You and sing*

*You're the God of the heavens
Of the sun, snow and rain
Cause my dreams to blossom
Like flowers in the spring*

*Grow Yourself a garden
With my words and with these songs
Shower me with inspiration
So the whole world may sing along*

Defrost ten thousand winters
Create love from bitterness
Let Your passion grow in my heart
'Til I see Your beautiful face

I was sound asleep,
but in my dreams I was wide awake.
Oh, listen! It's the sound of
my lover knocking, calling!

"Let me in, dear companion, dearest friend,
my dove, my consummate lover!
I'm soaked with the dampness of the night,
drenched with dew, shivering and cold."

Song of Solomon 5:2

Song 7

ಬಾ *Without You* ಲ್ಯ
Jesus Singing over His Bride

*I feel like a King without a country
And a Castle without a door
A Lover without a heart
Like a Warrior without a sword
Without you I am but a Fairytale
That happily never ends
Like a Knight without a princess
There's no one here to defend*

*I feel like a Song without a melody
And a Poem without a rhyme
A Romance without the love
Like a Toast without the wine
Without you I'm but a Groom
Who is aching for His bride
Like a Wedding without the guests
There's no one here by My side*

*I feel like a Boat without the ocean
And Sails without the wind
A Ship without a rudder
Like a Pirate who could never win
Without you I'm but a Raft
Lost in the middle of the sea
Like a Compass requires a needle
I need you here with Me*

I feel like the Earth without its orbit
And a Star without the light
The Sun without its shining
Like a Day without the night
Without you I'm but a Cloud
Blowing 'round without the sky
Like a Planet without a galaxy
I am missing you tonight

The kisses of your lips are honey, my love,
every syllable you speak a delicacy to savor.

Song of Solomon 4:11

Song 8

෨ *The Only Living God* ෬
The Bride Singing to Jesus

I never had a King
To love me like You before
I never dreamed of all the things
That You have for me in store
How do I begin to give You my praise?
I will worship You in eternity
And for the rest of my days
Blinded by my sin, fear and shame
Staring into the mirror
I am the only one to blame
Why didn't I listen, why couldn't I see
That all You ever had
Was a deep abiding love for me?
You asked me to surrender
And give You my heart
After all my dreams had shattered
And fallen all apart
I picked up the pieces
And held out my hand
An offering of brokenness
I had built upon the sand
You restored my heart
And made me whole
You gave me wings to fly
Deep within my soul
Therefore I will follow You

For the rest of my earthly life
Loving you passionately
Like an adoring wife
I will hang on Your every word
The ones that You breathe
For it is You alone that I worship
And will live to please
Your grace and Your mercy
They overwhelm me so
I'll shout it from the mountains
I want the whole world to know
That You alone
Are the only living God
There are no others
On this earth that we trod
I will live to call forth
The bride You have won
The bride of Christ
The virgins, the holy ones
Multiply my efforts
Like the fish and the bread
So that over Your enemies
Your kingdom will soon tread
Cause Your name
And Your glory to resound
So that those who are lost
Will all be found

*We'll celebrate, we'll sing, we'll make great music.
Yes! For your love is better than vintage wine.*

Song of Solomon 1:4

Song 9

☙ *Out of My Mind* ❧
Jesus Singing over His Bride

Sometimes I hear you speaking
Sometimes I can hear your voice in rhyme
Got Me thinking I'm crazy; out of My mind
Cause you're here in heaven
Even though you're gone
Here in heaven
Even though you're gone

Sometimes I hear you singing
An angelic voice that sounds divine
Got Me thinking about you all of the time
Cause you're here in heaven
Even though you're gone
Here in heaven
Even though you're gone

Sometimes I see your reflection
I turn around and I see you shine
Got Me thinking you're an angel of some kind
Cause you're here in heaven
Even though you're gone
Here in heaven
Even though you're gone

Sometimes I see your face
Seeing through a hole in time
Got Me thinking you're some kind of find
Cause you're here in heaven
Even though you're gone
Here in heaven
Even though you're gone

Can't you see
You've left your fingerprints all over me
All over this world
All over this heart of mine?
No matter what I do
I can't get you out of My mind
Cause you're here in heaven
Even though you're gone
Here in heaven
Even though you're gone

I can't get you out of My mind
Can't get you out
Cause you're here in heaven
Even though you are gone
Here in heaven
Even though you are gone

My lover has arrived and he's speaking to me.

Song of Solomon 2:10

Song 10

෨ *God's Voice* ଔ
The Bride Singing to Jesus

Adam heard God say,
"Don't eat the fruit of the good and evil bark."
God spoke to Noah,
"Go and build a giant gopher wood ark."
Abram heard, "Leave home to a new land
And I will give you a son."
God told Rebekah, "You shall have twins
And the older shall serve the younger one."
A voice came to Isaac,
"Don't go to Egypt but dwell in the land."
Jacob dreamed,
"I'll give you the land and your descendants will be
As numerous as the sand."
Joseph heard,
"One day your family will all bow down to you."
God told Pharaoh of Egypt,
"Seven years of famine could devastate you."
"I have come to deliver my people,"
Moses heard from a bush set ablaze.
Then God struck down Pharaoh
Bringing judgment through the plagues.
God commanded Joshua,
"Cross over the Jordan
And I will give you the promised land.
Don't be afraid, have courage; against you
No man will be able to stand."

A shepherd boy named David heard,
"I will make you a king."
While Isaiah heard, "Who will go for Me?
Who will stand for Me and sing?"
Joseph heard,
"Don't be afraid, take Mary as your wife.
She shall give birth to the Messiah
And he will live a sinless life."
At His baptism Jesus heard,
"Behold this is My beloved Son,
He will deliver the people from their sins,
For He is the Lamb; My chosen One."
Peter and Andrew were fishing by the sea,
When along came Jesus who said,
"Drop your nets, come and follow Me."
To the adulterous woman Jesus said,
"Go and sin no more.
"For I have delivered you from condemnation,
My love is your cure."
Then there's Matthew, Mark, Luke and John,
Who all heard the voice of Jesus,
The holy risen One.
And what of Paul,
Who was struck down from his high horse?
He heard, "I am Jesus whom you are persecuting,
You need to change your course."
Then there was Saint Augustine,
Joan of Arc and Martin Luther King,
All saints who heard the voice of God
So gloriously sing.
For all throughout history
You spoke and Your children heard,

For what You spoke was Your divine living word.
And when You speak You give us a choice,
To obey or not obey the sound of Your voice.
So if today I hear You, I won't harden my heart,
For that is what Adam and Eve did at the very start.

The night watchmen found me
as they patrolled the streets of the city.
They slapped and beat and bruised (my heart)...
these watchmen who were supposed
to be guarding the city.

Song of Solomon 5:7

Song 11

❧ *A Lifetime of Love* ☙
Jesus Singing over His Bride

How could a rose bloom without the thorns?
How could a butterfly soar without the struggle?
How could the garden grow
Without the thunderstorm?
How could a heart mend unless it's first broken?
How could a baby be born without pain?

A mother never hated her child
For the pain she endures to give birth
The pain subsides
And all that is left is a beautiful baby
A lifetime of love, joy and wonderful memories
Ready to be made

But before the love
Before the joy
Before the wonderful memories comes pain
Intense struggle and sorrow
And so it is with love

So hold on My Beloved
Hold on through the dark night
And never give up when your pain
is too much to bear
When your heart is torn
When you shed countless tears
And the sorrow consumes your soul

It's only a sign
Of the life that is coming
Of the love that is waiting to be born
Of all the joy that is waiting for you to hold
Of a lifetime of wonderful memories
That will be yours to make

His words are kisses, his kisses words.
Everything about him delights me,
thrills me through and through!
That's my lover, that's my man,
dear Jerusalem sisters.

Song of Solomon 5:16

Song 12

☙ *Amazing Love* ❧
The Bride Singing to Jesus

When I was alone and abandoned
You drew near to me
Broken and afraid
You set my imprisoned heart free

Dazed and confused
But drawn to Your light
I surrendered my heart
And You rescued me from my plight

I heard Your voice singing
As You rejoiced over me
You overwhelmed me with Your love
And gave me eyes to see

Amazing love, is it any wonder?
Amazing love, I am here to say
I'm so in love with You Jesus
I'm Yours for the rest of my days

You reached into my heart
Into the deepest parts of me
Filled me with Your presence
And gave me faith to believe

Your touch so tender
Your embrace so kind
Mending my brokenness
One piece at a time

Your love so extravagant
Your forgiveness so free
I can't help but worship You
For all eternity

Amazing love, is it any wonder?
Amazing love, I am here to say
I'm so in love with You Jesus
I'm Yours for the rest of my days

*No sooner had I left them than I found him,
found my dear lost love.
I threw my arms around him and held him tight,
wouldn't let him go until I had him home again,
safe at home beside the fire.*

Song Solomon 3:4

Song 13

༄ *Safe* ༄
Jesus Singing over His Bride

*When the storms of life are raging
And the waves are all you can see
Call on the name of Jesus
Then run and hide in Me
You're safe in My arms
Safe from harm you'll always be*

*I'll protect you in your storms
And calm your raging seas
Call on the name of Jesus
And put your trust in Me
You're safe in My arms
Your refuge I'll always be*

*When the thunder clouds are clashing
And lightening strikes the ground
Call on the name of Jesus
Then run and hide in Me
You're safe in My arms
Safe from harm you'll always be*

I'll turn your darkness to sunshine
And make the birds to sing
Call on the name of Jesus
And put your trust in Me
You're safe in My arms
Your refuge I'll always be

When your imagination is running wild
And the darkness brings you fear
Call on the name of Jesus
Then run and hide in Me
You're safe in My arms
Safe from harm you'll always be

I'll dispatch a thousand angels
To melt away your fears
Just call on the name of Jesus
And put your trust in Me
You're safe in My arms
Your refuge I'll always be

*Oh let me warn you, sisters in Jerusalem,
by the gazelles, yes, by all the wild deer:
Don't excite love, don't stir it up,
until the time is ripe – and you're ready.*

Song of Solomon 2:7

Song 14

෨ *The Heart of a Lion* ෬
The Bride Singing to Jesus

Justice is the calling
The day of salvation is Your plea
Binding up the brokenhearted
So that the lost will all be free

Roaming through the cities
Like a lion searching for prey
Devouring the darkness
Fear flees as You kneel to pray

The heart of a lion
Dwelling deep within
No fear of death
No slavery to sin

The faith in Your Father
Your trust like a child
A hand full of compassion
A heart completely wild

Shaking Your mane fiercely
Letting out a piercing roar
Destroying the gates of hell
The darkness screams, "No more!"

Love is Your motivation
In mercy You believe
Good news for the oppressed
Making the blind eyes see

Comforting the afflicted
Bringing gladness to those who weep
Singing praises where pain once dwelt
Awakening those who sleep

Courage is Your fortress
Divine words Your skillful sword
I'm standing on a mountaintop
Singing, "Jesus You're my Lord

There are no others
One God is He
Father, Son and Spirit
The Holy Trinity

All will bow and worship
The soon and coming King
But until You return
I will stand in the assembly and sing

Holy, Holy our God is One
Worthy, Worthy we worship the Son
Humbly, Humbly we bow before Your throne
Victory, Victory the battle You have won"

*You're so beautiful, my darling, so beautiful,
and your dove eyes are veiled
by your hair as it flows and shimmers...
Your smile is generous and full -
expressive and strong and clean.
Your lips are jewel red,
your mouth elegant and inviting,
your veiled cheeks soft and radiant.*

Song of Solomon 4:1-3

Song 15

❧ *If You Would Give Me This Dance* ☙
Jesus Singing over His Bride

*The night is young
The stars gleaming bright
Across the yard
I've been captivated by a light
The moon is glowing
Shining on your gorgeous face
Revealing stunning beauty
With such amazing grace*

*Alone you are sitting
Watching as others dance
Wondering, "Where is my prince?
When will I get my chance?"
All the while I've been dreaming of you
From across the lawn
Studying this game of chess
Before I move My first pawn*

*The band is playing
The lights are down low
I have fallen for an angel
But how do I let it show?
How should I approach her?
What's My opening line
To approach such beauty
An angel so divine?*

*Trembling, I stand to My feet
And walk across the yard
Rarely in My life have I done anything
Quite so hard
My heart is pounding
Uncertainty is what I feel
Am I just dreaming
Or are you truly real?*

*Delirious
I am standing by your side
Intense feelings
I am unable to hide
I stare into your eyes
Yours latch onto mine
They sparkle, "I've been waiting for you
All of this time."*

*Nervously I stretch out My hand
"Isn't tonight wonderful
And this affair so grand?
You are so beautiful
I couldn't resist the chance
To tell you that
All My dreams would come true
If you would give Me this dance."*

Come and look, sisters in Jerusalem.
Oh, sisters of Zion, don't miss this!
My King-Lover, dressed
and garlanded for his wedding,
his heart full, bursting with joy!

Song of Solomon 3:11

Song 16

꧁ *Lost in You* ꧂
The Bride Singing to Jesus

Lost in Your voice
Mesmerized by the sound
Bowing in silence before You
My face to the ground

Lost in Your beauty
Enraptured by what I see
Longing just to know You
More intimately

Lost in Your presence
It's where I long to be
Dwelling with You forever
To love You endlessly

Lost in Your heaven
Captured by Your embrace
Yearning just to hold You
To see You face to face

Lost in Your love
Enslaved without a key
I'm Your prisoner now
Yours for eternity

You've captured my heart, dear friend.
You looked at me, and I fell in love.
One look my way and I was hopelessly in love!

Song of Solomon 4:9

Song 17

❧ *Heaven on Earth* ☙
Jesus Singing over His Bride

What is it in your eyes
That keeps Me hypnotized?
What is it in your smile
That drives My heart so wild?
Could you tell Me your secret?
Or are you going to keep it?
Cause I don't know the answers
But I know one thing
You are My heaven
You are My heaven here on earth

What is it in your voice
That steals My will of its choice?
What is it about your walk
That puts My mind into shock?
Could you tell Me your secret?
Or are you going to keep it?
Cause I don't know the answers
But I know one thing
You are My heaven
You are My heaven here on earth

What is it about your love
That keeps pouring down from above?
What is it about you girl
That continually spins My world?
Could you tell Me your secret?
Or are you going to keep it?
Cause I don't know the answers
But I know one thing
You are My heaven
You are My heaven here on earth

When I need a glimpse of heaven
When I need to experience God's grace
I have found the secret
And I can't even keep it
I simply look into your eyes
And gaze upon your beautiful face
Then I know I have seen heaven
I have seen heaven here on earth

I beg you, sisters in Jerusalem -
if you find my lover,
Please tell him I want him,
that I'm heartsick with love for him.

Song of Solomon 5:8

Song 18

ೞ *Savior* ಜ
The Bride Singing to Jesus

*You are my Savior
That's what You are to me
The Anchor in my ocean
The North Star over my sea*

*When the storms of life are raging
And the waves are all I see
I will cry out to You my Savior
"Come and rescue me"*

*You are my Savior
Your face is all I seek
Seated high above all others
Savior to the meek*

*When the winds and waves are crashing
And I've lost my way within the night
I will trust in Your unfailing love
To lead me to Your light*

*You are my Savior
None other could compare
Awesome is the glory that surrounds You
All the saints bow in prayer*

Fill me with Your Spirit
Flow through me with Your love
I will love You all the days of my life
Giving the glory to God above

Dear, dear friend and lover,
you're as beautiful as Tirzah,
city of delights, lovely as Jerusalem,
city of dreams, the ravishing visions of my ecstasy.
Your beauty is too much for me –
I'm in over my head.

Song of Solomon 6:4-5

Song 19

෨ *Eternity* ଈ
Jesus Singing over His Bride

Let Me touch you gently
Let Me heal your heart
Let Me mend your brokenness
And take away your hurt
I'll give My tenderness
You'll tremble when we kiss
Oh Eternity
My love will heal your brokenness

I'll love you eternally
Breathless you will be
Ecstasy forever
If you surrender your heart to Me
No more crying
No more lonely nights
No more sad struggles
Or dark demons to fight

Let Me touch you gently
Let Me heal your heart
Let Me mend your brokenness
And take away your hurt
I'll give My tenderness
You'll tremble when we kiss
Oh Eternity
My love will heal your brokenness

*But my lover wouldn't take no for an answer,
and the longer he knocked,
the more excited I became.*

Song of Solomon 5:4

Song 20

ॐ *You are Love* ॐ
The Bride Singing to Jesus

You are my Healer
The Mender of my broken heart
The Hope of my Salvation
The One I have searched for from the start

You are the Water that I thirst for
The Heir of all things
The Light within my world
The Song that I sing

You are my Bread sent from heaven
The Ruler of the world
The Faithful and True Witness
The Living Word of God

You are the Bright Morning Star
The Joy within my soul
My Door and my Deliverer
The Salvation the world should know

You are my Advocate
The Almighty One
The Alpha and Omega
My Precious Cornerstone

You are my Hope of Glory
The Holy One and True
Salvation for the Gentiles
Salvation for the Jews

You are the Lamb without blemish
The Smile upon my face
The Home that I long for
My heart full of Grace

But most of all You are Love
Yes, Love is what you are to me
And this is the most important thing
That I want the whole world to see

*Oh, dear friend! You're so beautiful!
And your eyes so beautiful – like doves!*

Song of Solomon 1:15

Song 21

ಖ *Heaven in Your Eyes* ಜ
Jesus Singing over His Bride

*When I long to see heaven
All I do is look at you
Then My world starts spinning
As I am drawn to the light in your eyes
Then I know I have seen heaven
Heaven in your eyes*

*When I desire to hear an angel
All I do is listen to you
Then My heart beats anew
As I hear your beautiful voice
Then I know I have heard an angel
An angel in your voice*

*When I want to see a rainbow
All I do is gaze at you
Then my senses start to tingle
As I get lost in your amazing smile
Then I know I've found a rainbow
A rainbow in your smile*

When I aspire to smell a rose
All I do is breathe the scent of you
Then I catch My breath
As I smell the sweetness of you
Then I know I've smelt a rose
A rose in your scent

But when I opened the door, he was gone.
My loved one had tired of waiting and left.
And I died inside – oh, I felt so bad!
I ran out looking for him
but he was nowhere to be found.
I called into the darkness – but no answer.

Song of Solomon 5:6

Song 22

☙ *My Heart Let Me Find You* ❧
The Bride Singing to Jesus

*Lost in the darkness,
In fear completely alone
I was wandering this weary world
Trying to find my way home*

*Utter disappointment,
Sorrow, despair and pain
Broke my heart into pieces
In the end all my gain*

*Your love arose like the sunrise
Within my heart I found Your light
Guiding me through this dreary world
To be home with You my delight*

*Though I never knew You, Jesus
Though my eyes could not see
My heart let me find You
This side of eternity*

*Taken to the depths of Abaddon
To the bottom of the abyss
I found all manner of sin within me
I forsook You with a kiss*

Through great anguish
Deprivation and shame
My heart being shredded
No one but me to blame

Lost without reason
Tormented by fear
Your love still guiding me
I could feel You very near

Though I never knew You, Jesus
Though my eyes could not see
My heart let me find You
This side of eternity

Searching beyond reason
To fill this empty space
I needed You near me
I longed to feel Your embrace

I surrendered my search to find You
Stopped looking for the light
That is when I found You
In the depths of this cold night

Now I wait on Father
For His will to be done
Learning of grace and mercy
Pursuing Your kingdom come

Though I never knew You, Jesus
Though my eyes could not see
My heart let me find You
This side of eternity

For Your love was the answer
Your love removed my shame
Love is Who was leading me
Love is Your name

*Let me see your face, let me hear your voice.
For your voice is soothing
and your face is ravishing.*

Song of Solomon 2:14

Song 23

✥ *The Wedding Rehearsal: The Look Says It All* ✥
Jesus Singing over His Bride

*I walk into heaven and see My bride.
I can't help but stare at you through the clouds.
You gaze back at Me.
No words are exchanged.
The look says it all.*

*My eyes whisper,
"I love you and I will always love you."
You smile.
You read My eyes and know My every thought.
Your eyes speak to mine.
We have an intimate conversation without words.
My heart can read your thoughts.
Silently I mouth, "You are so beautiful."
You blush.
With a whimsical look I whisper again,
"No, I mean it."
Then a serious look reveals a deeper secret.
"I can't live without you."
You smile because you already know this.
I think to myself,
"I am the most fortunate man alive.
I would never take you for granted."
You can sense My overwhelming appreciation
for you without words.*

My heart sings,
"You are the greatest treasure of all."
You feel deeply cherished.
You begin to glow.
My Spirit intermingles with your spirit
through the clouds.
We drink of a deep refreshing spring of love.
It's intense, passionate, life-giving and enduring.
All of heaven's angels watch our communion.
And they are astonished by our love.
The wedding rehearsal begins.

I walk into heaven and see My bride.
I can't help but stare at you through the clouds.
You stare back at Me.
No words are exchanged.
The look says it all.

*I am my lover's. I'm all he wants.
I'm all the world to him.*

Song of Solomon 7:10

Song 24

ೞ *The Vows: I Belong to You* ☙
The Bride Singing to Jesus

I belong to You
I belong to You
You lavish me with Your love
You were sent here from heaven
And left Your Father above

Abandoned Your throne in glory
Stooped down to earth for me
Opened these blinded eyes
And gave me liberty

You belong to me
You belong to me
I love You with all my heart
I will live for You forever
Never shall we part

You shower me with devotion
And have become my destiny
Removed these bitter chains
And set my broken heart free

*I belong to You
I belong to You
You lavish me with Your love
You were sent here from heaven
And left Your Father above*

*I will love You forever
Stand and proclaim Your fame
Tell the whole world of Your greatness
And sing of Your holy name*

*You belong to me
You belong to me
I love You with all my heart
I will live for You forever
Never shall we part*

All I want to do is sit in his shade,
To taste and savor his delicious love.
He took me home with him for a festive meal,
but his eyes feasted on me!

Song of Solomon 2:3-4

Song 25

ও *The Marriage: Intimacy* ର
Jesus and the Bride Singing Together in Heaven

One heart
One choice
One will
One voice

You are the love within
The grace that I seek
You are my hope of heaven
And my faith to believe

You are my intimacy
All of your love for me
Made these blind eyes see
You are the only one for me

One song
One mind
One soul
One rhyme

You are my ears to hear
And my eyes to see
You are the words that I savor
And the song that I sing

You are my intimacy
All of your love for me
Made these blind eyes see
You are the only one for me

One smile
One kiss
One spirit
One bliss

You are the touch that I long for
And the embrace that I need
You are the one who I cherish
And the soul who sets me free

You are my intimacy
All of your love for me
Made these blind eyes see
You are the only one for me

Kiss me - full on the mouth! Yes!
For your love is better than wine,

Song of Solomon 1:2

A New Song

*Sing to the Lord a new song;
Sing to the Lord, all the earth.
Sing to the Lord, praise His name;
Proclaim His salvation day after day.
Declare His glory among the nations,
His marvelous deeds among all peoples.
For great is the Lord and most worthy of praise;
He is to be feared above all gods.*

Psalm 96:1-4 (NIV)

✼ What's Next? ✼

We invite you to continue your journey with *The Divine Romance: The Song of Jesus and His Bride* at either:

www.trueloveconsulting.com
or
www.myspace.com/trueloveconsulting

~ *Share your feelings about The Divine Romance and read what others are saying*
~ *Read David's blog*
~ *Purchase additional copies to share with your friends*
~ *Discover what's next*
~ *Learn how a portion of the proceeds from this book are donated to sponsor the needs of children through the ministry of Compassion International.*

www.ingramcontent.com/pod-product-compliance
Lightning Source LLC
LaVergne TN
LVHW041710060526
838201LV00043B/663